Jokers Dressed Up As Kings:

Toxic Traits in a Relationship

Monaca Vanderpool

Jokers Dressed Up As Kings

Toxic Traits in Relationships

ISBN: 9798329207996

Publisher: **Marissa F. Cohen**

www.PublishWithMarissa.com

Publication Date: July, 2024

Cover Design: Angie Ayala

Photographer: Colleen Megan

Special Quantity Discounts

Retail: $19.97

5-20 Books	$16.97
21-99 Books	$14.97
100-499 Books	$11.97
500-999 Books	$8.97
1000+ Books	$7.97

WWW.MONACAVANDERPOOL.COM

Special Quantity Discounts on Journals

Retail: $11.97

5-20 Journals	$10.97
21-99 Journals	$9.97
100-499 Journals	$8.97
500-999 Journals	$6.97
1000+ Journals	$5.97

WWW.MONACAVANDERPOOL.COM

GLITCH MOB PODCAST

WHERE REAL STORIES, INSIGHTS, AND CONVERSATIONS COME TO LIFE. JOIN YOUR HOST, MONACA VANDERPOOL, A SINGLE MOM, ENTREPRENEUR, AND A BELIEVER IN THE POWER OF RESILIENCE AND TRANSFORMATION. AT GLITCH MOB, WE TEAR OFF THE VEIL OF PERFECTION TO SHARE THE RAW, THE REAL, AND THE TRULY LIFE-CHANGING STORIES. WHETHER YOU'RE A SINGLE PARENT, A BUDDING ENTREPRENEUR, OR SOMEONE WHO'S SIMPLY SEEKING INSPIRATION AMIDST LIFE'S CHAOS, YOU'VE FOUND YOUR TRIBE. WE'LL CHAT WITH INCREDIBLE GUESTS, SHARE ACTIONABLE INSIGHTS, AND, MOST IMPORTANTLY, WE'LL DO IT TOGETHER, AS A COMMUNITY THAT UPLIFTS AND EMPOWERS. IT'S TIME TO EMBRACE THE GLITCH AND FIND THE BEAUTY IN THE BREAKDOWNS.

WWW.MONACAVANDERPOOL.COM

WITH MONACA VANDERPOOL

Dedication:

To my Tribe—you know who you are—thank you for being there every day and helping me close the chapter. I love you more than words can express and would not be where I am without you.

To my readers, if you ever find yourself in the wrong story, leave. You're allowed to leave any story you don't find yourself in. You're allowed to leave any story you don't love yourself in. You're allowed to let toxic relationships go, to surround yourself with love and people who encourage and nurture you. You're allowed to pick the kind of energy you need in your life. You're allowed to look in the mirror and like what you see.

And lastly, to those who will say I'm "playing the victim", if you decide to read this book, I hope you read it with an open heart.

> You are not a victim for sharing your story.
>
> You are a survivor setting the world on fire with your truth.
>
> And you never know who needs your light, your warmth,
>
> and raging courage.
>
> -Alex Elle

Contents

Foreword:

Dear Monaca, 2011,

Prepare yourself; this is going to hurt – a lot. You are about to meet your 'Knight in Shining Armor'. He's going to sweep you off your feet and it's going to make you feel like you have met your soulmate. You will believe that for 13 years.

You will make a lot of memories with this person. Memories that won't be erased, no matter how hard you try. Whether you like it or not, they will be a part of your story. The two of you joined paths for a reason, and you will walk through some of the hardest times together. Brace yourself; for there will be infidelity, betrayal, and divorce. There are going to be several periods when you're going to feel lost and broken, and believe that you are not enough. You will even become angry at God. Why me?

It's going to be a strange feeling having someone in your life for 13 years, and then one day, poof! They are suddenly not there anymore. It will be bizarre how your relationship will change so vast and rapidly. When you come out the other side, you will understand that God knew you could handle it and He brought you through it to bring you here.

We are going to share your story, so that you can inspire others found in similar situations. We will only share those "red flag" stories, in hopes of giving your reader the knowledge and inspiration they will need. Your honest approach to what you will have to live with is going to give them a road map on how to handle any bumps in the road to their recovery and freedom.

In telling your story, you'll have to become vulnerable and transparent about things you've tried to hide and keep under the covers for so many years. Be honest and don't hold anything back. Our intentions are not to hurt or 'label' anyone. For this reason alone, their names will be changed.

You are in such a good place now, you are happy, and you are thriving. You feel like you can finally be yourself. It's okay that your heart will still hurt occasionally because of what happened. I need you to know that you will not feel this way forever. You will move forward, and you will continue to grow with every day that passes. You may not be at peace with what happened between the two of you, and that is perfectly fine. Sometimes, the people you wanted as part of your story, are only meant to be a chapter, and you are only meant to be their #1 T-shirt girl.

Keep your head up,

Monaca, 2024

Chapter 1:

How You Get the Girl

#1 T-shirt Place.
These smell better than your azalea's.
Have a good day.
Dinner Soon!
Promise.

Standing outside my office with a grin from ear to ear, butterflies in my stomach, and a racing heart, I read the card attached to the most beautiful bouquet of flowers I had ever seen. I thought to myself, "Who is this guy? I met him yesterday, and in less than 24 hours, he has stirred up feelings in me that I've never felt before." I'm not sure what it was about him, but it attracted me to him. And so the story begins...

Living in a cute 3-bedroom house, nestled on half an acre in the woods of an older neighborhood (close to my parents, of course) it was me, my 2 children, and my promotional company that I had started in my breakfast nook in 2007. I was a single mom who was in her groove and loving life. My plans were to never marry again and to put everything I had into my kids and my business, and I was doing just that. The kids were happy, we loved where we lived, and my promotional company was soaring! Especially after I made the decision to move into an office outside my house, to start bringing on Sales Reps, and to purchase equipment to begin

3

in-house production. I had a large network of friends and business colleagues and was a social butterfly. Life was good.

June 15, 2011, changed my plans. That was the day that Clyde walked into my front lobby and that was where our '615' journey started. We had a 1:15pm meeting scheduled that day for him to order shirts. We immediately had a strong attraction to each other. I followed through with my normal spiel about screen print and embroidery and walked him through my showroom so he could see samples. I could feel the weight of his stare the entire time, and at one point he was so close to me I thought he was coming in for a kiss. Our meeting ended and I went about my day.

The flowers arrived the next day, and Clyde's charm kicked into high gear. I remember calling him "My Knight in Shining Armor". The first year was absolutely perfect. We spent hours and hours talking on the phone, texting, and hanging out on my back deck. We learned so much about each other – our childhoods, our favorite things, our favorite places, our future plans – he talked about it all. He was around for everything; he was there whenever I needed him, and said all the right things. We spent hours and hours together, talking and laughing. He was always interested in what I was doing; he wanted to know my friends, colleagues, customers... everyone. He was so into me, and it made me feel like I was his #1. His 'take charge' energy and confidence turned me on, it was very masculine to me.

"This is too good to be true," I said to myself many times. Eventually, I was convinced that this must be what it feels like to find your soulmate.

"Just want you to know I love you very much!"

Another bouquet of flowers just arrived. He just got better and better. More butterflies... and he loves me now! We started saying 'I love you' within the first month. Life was intoxicating.

Immediately, he started helping wherever he could at my promotional company. He learned the ins and outs of everything. He met all my customers, worked with my sales reps, and even helped with production. He took charge. So hot! There were several evenings I would leave to get the kids and he would stay to make sure things got done. Everyone was being taken care of. It was the perfect fit, and he'd come home at night. If he didn't have his child, he stayed at my house. Yes, we were becoming a blended family, and holy shit, I found out he was married. This was something I didn't find out until several weeks after we met. Clyde had told me that he was going through a divorce, so naturally I figured that was already in process. It wasn't until one afternoon his wife came into my office to introduce herself that I knew he was still married and was still living with her. I was not proud of how that played out. Hurting another woman was never something I imagined would come out of that. Since then, she and I have made amends, and we respect each other. She is beautiful and tough and an amazing person.

RED FLAG

Clyde and I started traveling together—both business and pleasure. He would go with me to trade shows, we would plan weekend trips, and I started taking him to work events with me. It was exciting and our time together was intense and romantic. Yes, the sex was a-ma-zing and completely insane; we did it at every chance we had. We even took a 'ride' on the Monorail at Disney World. We didn't care where we were—we called anyone around us "ornaments" (meaning the world was just about him and me, and everything else didn't bother us).

Needless to say, Clyde and I settled into a serious relationship quickly. Our word was "forever". We said it with every chance we could. We loved each other intensely and knew at the time that we would be together "forever". How fucking cute is that?

15 months later, HE PROPOSED! Of course, I said yes! He was my knight in shining armor, right?

Love Bombing

An attempt to influence a person by demonstrations of attention and affection. It can be used in different ways and for either positive or negative purposes. Psychologists have identified love bombing as a possible part of a cycle of abuse and have warned against it.

A sign of love bombing is being intensely showered with affection, gifts, and promises for the future with the predator so that the victim feels or is made to believe that it is a sign of "love at first sight".

Since things are going so perfectly, why not move into a house that fits all 5 of us? It made sense at the time. We moved into a rental house the next year and were feeling like a cute and cozy little family. The promotional company was kicking ass, the weekend trips continued, and the sex was even more intense.

Clyde loved to gamble, and we would drive to Charlestown quite often to play at the casino. We started with a small budget and would be sure to walk away if we lost what we came with. Twenty-five cent Quick Hit machines were our jam at first. Then, he taught me how to play Roulette and I fell in love with it. Soon after, he started booking private planes to Atlantic City and we would spend weekends at Caesars Palace, eating in fancy restaurants, shopping the outlets, and hitting the tables until all hours of the night. He loved buying me Coach purses, and he would gift them to me often. I played the roulette table and Clyde would stand close by and smoke cigarettes. We would 'stack on 15', because that was 'our number.' It was extremely exhilarating when 15 hit. There were several times we would walk away with thousands of dollars after a hit. When the night was over, we would head to the room and make love all night. Life was fun and action-packed.

a sense of superiority, uniqueness, or invulnerability that is unrealistic, and not based on personal capability. It may be expressed by exaggerated beliefs regarding one's abilities— the belief that few other people have anything in common with oneself, and that one can only be understood by a few, very special people. The personality trait of grandiosity is principally associated with narcissistic personality disorder (NPD).

1.   *The person exaggerates talents, capacity, and achievements in an unrealistic way.*

2.   *The person has grandiose fantasies.*

3.   *The person believes that they do not need other people.*

4.   *The person over-examines and downgrades other people's projects, statements, or dreams in an unrealistic manner.*

5.   *The person regards themself as unique or special when compared to other people.*

6.   *The person regards themself as generally superior to other people.*

7.   *The person behaves self-centeredly and/or self-referentially.*

8.   *The person behaves in a boastful or pretentious way.*

The Cycle of Narcissistic Abuse

This is a pattern of harmful behaviors used by someone with narcissistic traits to manipulate and exploit another person. The cycle is emotionally devastating and includes the following stages:

1. *Idealization or Love-Bombing*

2. *Devaluation*

3. *Discard*

4. *Hoovering or Re-engagement*

By maneuvering through these stages, the abuser gains a sense of power and control over the victim's emotions, thoughts, and behaviors. It creates a persistent state of dependency within the victim.

Chapter 2:

Tilted Stage

A couple of years had passed, and at this time, we were juggling 3 kids (all under the age of 10) and the work (Clyde worked for a small construction company and was still helping with the promotional business), and we fit in our time together when we could. If the kids were away, we made every point to have our date nights.

So, here we go. Monaca, take a deep breath.

Date night! One of my favorite restaurants was Bonefish Grill. Clyde wasn't a big seafood person, but he liked when I was happy; he would find something on the menu that he could eat anyway. This night was a usual night of dinner and drinks. Upon returning home, an argument developed. I don't remember exactly what we were fighting about—probably something trivial. But what I do remember is that this was the first time I remember him yelling with so much rage and screaming directly in my face. I asked him to stop, but that only fueled his rage. The only thing I knew to do was leave. So, I grabbed my keys, hopped in my truck and before I could put it in reverse, I felt a cold sensation in my lap. Clyde was pouring an entire beer on my lap as I was crying in my truck, trying to get away from him. WTH just happened? I saw a rage in his eyes that I had never seen before, and it scared me. I drove to Mom & Dad's house, grabbed a pair of my dad's pajama pants so I could take my beer-soaked pants off, went straight to my room and fell asleep (yes, I still have a room at my parents' house). Mom tried to talk to me, Dad tried to call me (he was out of town working), but all I wanted to do was go to sleep. I was humiliated. Those butterflies still existed, but they weren't the excited ones.

The next day, he apologized. I went to work and tried to forget the night happened.

RED FLAG

One of the best parts of our relationship was the relationship I got to build with his cool-ass family. LOVE, LOVE, LOVE, LOVE—all of them. I love the memories of when I met them. We traveled 3 states away and attended family parties, graduations, and weddings.

It was the night before a wedding, we left the rehearsal dinner and Clyde wanted to introduce me to some of his spots and friends. So, his parents and brother went home with Clyde's son, and we hit the town. It was a great evening—time with family, lots of cocktails, and reminiscing with his friends. When the night was over, per our norm, Clyde wanted to have sex. We stayed at his parents' house; our room was right next to theirs, and that was a line I didn't want to cross. I would be mortified if his mom woke up to us having sex. So, I told him "No". The next thing I remember was me being on the floor, trying to find the glasses that flew off my face when he pushed me across the bed. My body was shaking in fear as I stood up and pushed past him. The thump from my body hitting the wall woke his brother. He came around the corner as I was walking out of the room, and he ran into Clyde, face-to-face. The two of them immediately started yelling and pushing each other. All the commotion woke their parents, and they came around the corner wondering what was going on. It was then that Clyde turned around and met his stepdad, face-to-face, screaming and pushing up against his chest. It all happened so fast and was so intense. I was crying hysterically at this point and jumped in my car to leave. Unaware of where I was going, I sat in my car for a few minutes to calm down. All I could think about was Clyde's child sleeping on the couch. I couldn't leave him, so I stepped back into the house, swooped him up and carried him into the back bedroom and locked the door. My only thoughts were to keep him safe and away from what was happening in the living room.

Clyde's parents called 911, and as soon as the police were called, Clyde ran out of the house. We locked the doors and got ourselves together. The rage that I saw was like nothing I had ever seen before. It was like he 'saw red', and nothing on this earth could calm him down. I tried to sleep that night but didn't have much success. About an hour after the incident, Clyde came knocking on the window for me to let him in, but I wouldn't.

I almost drove back home that night, but I didn't. I knew it meant so much to the bride for him to be there. The next morning, he came back to his parents' house, I looked him in the eyes and said "I know you didn't do it on purpose; I forgive you. Now let's go to the wedding and have a great time". We did just that; we had an absolute blast. We danced for the first time that night, and he was an absolute gentleman. Later, we would discover that our son was conceived that night, making that wedding one I would never forget, for many reasons. Again, WTH just happened?

RED FLAG

When I look back on our 13 years together, several of my memories are clouded by the sounds of yelling. The yells would escalate quickly, and in several instances, would end with Clyde directly in my face. He flew into these blind rages. My reaction was always to shut down. I knew I could never reason with him, calm him down, or get away from him. So many times, I would beg him, "Please stop… please stop… please stop." He never would. So then, I stayed silent and closed my eyes, which made him even angrier. I remember times when I would pull the covers over my head and he would rip them off me. He wanted to make sure I was listening to him, and even wanted me to look him in the face. The times when he left me there in the fetal position, with no covers, made me feel like I was nothing. I then started to run into the bathroom and lock the door to get away from him. He always knew how to unlock the door. He would come into the bathroom and close the door behind him, trapping me in. It was awful.

One of the worst moments was when he ripped a "Trophy Wife" shirt right off me on our wedding night while screaming in my face. His rage was so intense, he had the strength to tear my shirt straight down the middle with his bare hands. We were on a cruise at the time, and I had nowhere to go. I ended up sleeping in my brother's room that night.

His intimidation was so intense, on several occasions I had to call 911. It was the only thing that would make him stop. Every time, he left before the police arrived. The short time that the officers stood at my door to check on me were the only moments I felt safe when Clyde was in that rage. There was a time when I had to look at our son and ask him to call 911 because Clyde had snatched my phone out of my hand. He was 8-years old at the time. It was heart-wrenching.

SO MANY RED FLAGS

Devaluation

The reduction or underestimation of the worth or importance of something. A behavior exhibited by individuals with NPD where they denigrate, belittle, or dismiss others in order to maintain their own sense of superiority and self-importance.

While idealization places a person, place, or thing on a pedestal, devaluation refers to the act of assigning exaggerated negative qualities, while disregarding the good. During devaluation, flaws, weaknesses, and negative traits take center stage, and positive qualities are completely ignored.

Rage

An intense, uncontrolled anger that is an increased stage of hostile response to a perceived egregious injury or injustice. Rage is from C. 1300, meaning 'madness, insanity; a fit of frenzy; rashness, foolhardiness, intense or violent emotion, anger, wrath; fierceness in battle; violence'.

Rage can sometimes lead to a state of mind where the individuals experiencing it believe they can do, and often are capable of doing things that may normally seem physically impossible. Those experiencing rage usually feel the effects of high adrenaline levels in the body. This increase in adrenal output raises the physical strength and endurance levels of the person and sharpens their senses, while dulling the sensation of pain. High levels of adrenaline impair memory.

A person in a state of rage may also lose much of their capacity for rational thought and reasoning, and may usually act violently, on their impulses, to the point that they may attack until they have been incapacitated, or the source of their rage has been destroyed, or otherwise removed.

Intimidation

A behavior and legal wrong which usually involves deterring or coercing an individual by threat of violence. This includes intentional behaviors of forcing another person to experience general discomfort such as humiliation, embarrassment, inferiority, limited freedom, etc. Intimidation is done to make the other person submissive (also known as cowing), to destabilize/undermine the other, to force compliance, to hide one's insecurities, to socially valorize oneself, etc.

Chapter 3:

Swimming in a Champagne Sea

God put it on my heart in 2007 to start my own business. I remember sitting at the kitchen table with my dad, telling him that I was going to quit my salaried position (a great-paying position) and start a commission-only job as a promotional product sales rep. I was a single mom of a 5-year-old, living with my parents, and paying the mortgage on a house I owned in Tennessee that had been destroyed by a tornado (long story). He looked at me and, with a deep voice, said "Monaca Adell" *(I knew he meant business when he called me Monaca Adell, and not 'Sissy Girl')*, "Monaca Adell, you're out of your mind. Not a good idea!" It was the only time I didn't listen to him (regarding business). I told him that something was stirring in my spirit, and I had to do it. I did just that.

By 2010, I had grown my company to a million-dollar company; it was my 'baby.' My days consisted of dropping my kids off at school and daycare (my beautiful baby girl entered this world in 2008), hitting the streets, mingling around in the networking circuit, placing orders, delivering the goods, running the books, and making my customers happy. Grab the kids, make dinner, homework, baths, and bedtime. Then I would get up the next day to do it all over again. I thrived in every environment I was in. My life was flowing, and I was loving every minute of it.

When Clyde came into my life in 2011, it was a bonus for him to help. He didn't know the industry, but he taught himself what he could, and I showed him the ropes to the best of my knowledge. He's an extremely motivated person; very smart, confident, and bold. He 'settled in' quickly.

He became very interested in knowing everyone I knew—my customers, my vendors, and people in my network. At the time, I didn't mind. I was an open book, and he had a great personality that 'connected' with everyone. My business continued to grow, which caused the workload to increase. There were several nights when Clyde would stay at the office to get things done while I went home to take care of the kids.

A few months later, I started noticing that he knew stuff I never told him. He knew about past conversations I had with friends—conversations that happened on Messenger, some of which were intimate. There was a particular conversation I had with an old friend about a Viking fantasy; something that only he and I talked about it. Clyde brought up 'Vikings' in the bedroom one evening and it caught me off guard. There was another incident where I had posted about donuts on my social media; it was a picture of donuts with a quote from Clark Gable, "Don't let it soak too long." Clyde started accusing me of sending 'subliminal messages' to an old boyfriend. It was so random and odd. Well, I found out that while he was at the office working late and I was at home with the kids, he was logging into my social media accounts and reading my messages. WTH!

RED FLAG

We found out that I was pregnant in 2013. Round 3 for me. All my pregnancies were rough, but this one topped the cake. I was so sick. If I was awake, I was sick; it was horrible. At one point, Clyde took me to my parents' house because he didn't know what else to do to help me. With me being down for the count, Clyde stepped up in my place with the promotional company. He took charge of the sales reps, the employees, the customers, and the suppliers.

Several months passed, I was still deathly ill, and I assumed everything at work was running smoothly. I remember getting a phone call from one of my top sales reps, telling me that she was leaving. A week later, my screen printer followed suit. What was happening? The only thing my rep would tell me is that she couldn't work with him. To this day, I've never had the heart to tell Clyde that. It wasn't a good feeling.

With the baby coming soon and knowing that Clyde and I would be together 'forever,' we made a bold decision to shut down the promotional company and start a construction business. It made sense, right? He had a construction background, and I knew the business side of things. So, in 2014, our construction business was born.

I thrive in change; I believe I developed this trait from growing up in the military. I absolutely love the excitement and risk of it all. This was when I learned that Clyde liked it too. We became a 'Power Team'. The business grew, and it grew very fast. It became a huge part of who we were. Most of our conversations began centering on the business, even during our dates.

We were about 3 years into it and were focusing on the residential side of things. There were waves of work that would come and go. It was then that my ex-husband, who was working for a large hospital in the area, approached me and mentioned the need for contractors in the healthcare industry.

Side note: I have wonderful relationships with my previous husbands. We learned early on that it was not about us, but about the kids, and we all respect each other, to this day.

Anyway, when I discussed the healthcare industry with Clyde, he wasn't having any of it. He always brushed me off. It wasn't until we had a truck repossessed, and we were so desperate for money, that he entertained the idea. I guess being connected to my ex-husband in that sense was a hard pill for him to swallow. We needed a stream of revenue and that was our answer; beggars can't be choosers.

RED FLAG

That was the best decision we made for the business (thank you, ex-hubby). Once we stepped foot in the hospital and clinics, things started to explode. Everything moved so quickly, and we were saying 'yes' to jobs before we were equipped to handle them. What we did was book it, and then figure it out; it always worked out.

I noticed that my days consisted of dropping the kids off at school and daycare (including my stepchild, who I was blessed with the opportunity to help raise), going to the office, and staying at the office until work ended. I would then take care of any afternoon sports and homework with the kids, make dinner, get the kids ready for bed, and end my day. I wasn't networking, I wasn't going to the office, and I wasn't interacting with contractors, customers, or employees (besides my office staff). I was told that it 'wouldn't look good if anyone found out my connection to my ex-husband'. It made me feel very isolated and alone.

Speaking of isolation, this was the time that the 'Coronavirus' hit the states. Good 'ole Covid-19... What a whirlwind for us. With being in healthcare construction, all eyes were on us. It was another period of intense change, in which we thrived. We were transforming dorms into hospitals, erecting testing sites, creating 'Covid ICU Rooms'—you name it, we were doing it. We were also building our dream home at the same time. Life was fast and action-packed, just how we liked it.

Covid began to slow down, as did our construction business. It was another period of transition for us. We moved into the world of house flipping as the 'subcontractor.' This opened the opportunity to expand into other states. It was something that I never had peace about, and we could never put our finger on how to turn in the profits we were making in the past. Something was 'off.' It was the first time that Clyde started making decisions on his own (I'm talking about big decisions). Normally, we would discuss things together, and if both of us agreed, we would proceed. Not anymore.

RED FLAG

Isolation

The near or complete lack of social contact by an individual. Isolating targeted victims enables a narcissist to better manipulate and control them. When it comes to their partner and children, they isolate them from the outside world, from one another, and even from their own sense of reality. They want to keep you to themselves, so that they can control you and every aspect of your life. They also want to keep your attention focused solely on them. There is no room for anyone else in your life.

Financial Dependence

Reliance on others for income. A narcissist may downplay your income or devalue the work you do, making you feel inadequate or dependent on them. They may force you to quit your job or prevent you from working, making you dependent on their financial support.

I was extremely close with my dad; he was my hero, and I would move mountains to have him back. God took him home on April 16, 2020. He suffered from Idiopathic Pulmonary Fibrosis that he contracted from his time in the military. Once he was diagnosed, he flew out to Denver, CO, to go through testing at their Pulmonary Hospital. During a routine procedure, he coded. For 7 minutes, the nurses and doctors performed CPR and brought him back. I got on the next flight to Denver. I stayed with him for a few weeks, until he had the strength to fly back home. During my stay, I was surprised that I never heard from anyone. I never got a text or phone call from any of our family or friends. Very strange.

I found out later that Clyde had instructed everyone to contact him instead of "bothering Monaca." None of the messages ever got back to me. Hearing from family & friends would have been a welcomed distraction and comforting for both me and Dad. This made me feel isolated and controlled.

'*****'

Chapter 4:

A Circus isn't a Love Story

There is no denying that Clyde and I had an incredible sexual connection. Since day one, sex was something that we enjoyed and were good at. No matter where we were or how mad we were at each other, we never let anything get in the way of us making love to each other. It was incredible.

About 3 years into our relationship, right before his emotional affair with 'Ms. Texas Two Step' (I'll explain about her in Chapter 6), he started sharing his fantasy of watching me with another man. He would bring it up while we were having sex, and I didn't pay much attention to it at first. Eventually, he started asking me (outside of the bedroom) if I would consider it. My answer was 'abso-effing-lutely not!' (Excuse my language). Being intimate with another man was against everything I believed in. I am a God-fearing woman, and I cringed at the thought of what God would think of me. I believe that our marriage was sacred and the bedroom was for us only.

In my pursuit of becoming the perfect wife and the 'woman of Clyde's dreams', I did something I NEVER thought I would do. At this point, we are only a few months past his affair with the chick in Texas. Well, that thought stuck in my mind for several months, and I was getting to the point where I would do anything to make him happy, including putting my own beliefs aside.

RED FLAG

Date night! An evening opened for us to go on a date (at this point, it didn't happen often). Like clockwork, plans were to go out to dinner, have a few drinks, and get our freak on. We never ventured too far from that (no comment). As soon as we returned home, Clyde started planting the seed for us to 'invite a friend over'. After 3 martinis and an affair, I said, "Why the heck not?" This will save our marriage. I'll give my husband what he's been wanting and it'll bring us closer. Here we go.

The doorbell rang and the 3 of us headed straight to the bedroom. There was no beating around the bush; his 'guest' and I got right into it. A voice cried out in the back of my head, repeatedly, "Don't do it, Monaca; don't do it." I wish I would have listened to her, but I ignored the voice, and continued to do what I thought would help fix our marriage. It was horrible, and I had to fake it the entire time. At one point, I remember physically rolling my eyes because I wanted it to be over. Finally, he finished, Clyde finished, and the night ended.

I found out later that Clyde recorded the entire thing, without telling me.

RED FLAG

I also found out that I contracted an STD from the event. I'll spare you all those details, but if that wasn't God's way of telling me I made the wrong decision, I don't know what is. After sharing my doctor's appointment with Clyde, he brushed it off and acted like it wasn't a big deal. He did manage to pick me up from the hospital after my 'small procedure' was complete. He dropped me off at my parent's house so that I could recover there.

Sadly, time passed, and I agreed to another threesome. It was just as horrible as the first time. Obviously, it did not fix the marriage.

My point of sharing these stories is that I reached a low point where I was compromising my own values and beliefs for someone else—something I thought I would never do, but strangely felt right at the time because I was "in agreement" with my husband. To this day, I still have trouble forgiving myself for the abortion he wanted me to have. I haven't forgotten. I took his demons and made them mine. My love was completely blind, deaf, and dumb.

Clyde brought up the scenario of another man being with me pretty much every time we had sex. I got to the point where I didn't want to make love to him. I didn't want to think about being with another guy, but I knew that he would inevitably bring it up every time. How exhausting.

Our time in the bedroom would sometimes become 'aggressive'. At first, I didn't mind it. It was the moments when I had to tell him to 'be easy' that bothered me, because most of the time, he wouldn't listen to me. I slowly started to enjoy sex less and less.

RED FLAG

Apparently, there's such a thing as a mobile masseuse who will come to your house and give you a "full body" massage with a 'happy ending.' There was a period when Clyde repeatedly tried to convince me to do it. I found naked pictures of me on his computer where he had blurred out my face. He sent these pictures to the massage therapist when he was trying to set up the meeting, and he did so without my permission, obviously. No happy ending for me!

RED FLAG

'*****'

Triangulation

Intentionally introducing a third party, such as a friend, an ex-partner, or a family member, into a relationship. This third party serves as a tool for the narcissist to create a sense of competition, jealousy, and insecurity within the victim.

Control

Behavior used by the abusive person to gain and/or maintain control over another person. Manipulators and abusers may control their victims with a range of tactics, including, but not limited to, positive reinforcement (such as love bombing, praise, charm), negative reinforcement, intermittent or partial reinforcement, psychological punishment (such as silent treatment, threats, intimidation, guilt trips) and traumatic tactics (such as verbal abuse or explosive anger).

A common trait of narcissism is manipulative or controlling behavior. A narcissist will at first try to please and impress you, but eventually, their own needs will come first.

Chapter 5:

He Should've Said No

It was 3:22 am. I rarely wake up in the middle of the night, especially for no reason. The kids were sound asleep and there were no noises that would have woken me. I'm sure it was my angel nudging me. When I woke, I noticed that Clyde wasn't home yet. Although he worked late most nights (which I always found odd), this was a little excessive. So, like any other wife, I called my husband to see what was going on.

RING – BEEP. RING – BEEP. RING – BEEP

That's weird. Who would he be talking to at this time of the night? Once again, like any other concerned wife, I called him again. This time I got an answer. When I asked who he was speaking to, his first response was that he was talking to one of our employees. Liar, liar, pants on fire! Immediately I called bullshit on that. Come on! I was born at night, but not last night. Eventually, he confessed and admitted he was talking to a girl from Texas. WTH? I'll spare you the details of how he connected with this chick. He told me that he had been talking to her for a few weeks and that 'it didn't mean anything'. He was introduced to her while I was out of town on business. I remember he had flowers delivered to my hotel room, and even encouraged me to take a later flight coming home because he wanted me to 'enjoy being away'. There were those damn butterflies again.

Obviously in shock, I had so many questions about this emotional affair that he was having, one of them being, "Can you stop talking to her and delete her number?" He said that he had to think about it.

RED FLAG

I reacted in a way that I never thought I would have in this situation. I imagine that I would have said "Peace the-eff out" if I ever found my husband cheating. That's the type of woman I saw myself as. Instead, my reaction was, 'OMG, what have I not done as a wife to make him do this? Have I not been supportive enough? Do I not make him feel comfortable and loved when he gets home? Am I not cooking and doing his laundry enough? Am I not taking care of everything like I should?" It honestly makes me a little sick to my stomach to think of the way I reacted to him cheating for the first time.

I can't remember how long it took, but he eventually stopped talking to her (I assume). I do remember moments when I would talk to him on the phone and he would tell me he was waiting for her phone call. So, I would hang up, knowing that he would be talking to her soon, while I went about my day, working and taking care of the kids. We managed to get through that incident. I had to learn how to forgive and forget–one of the hardest things I've had to do. However, I did it.

Fast forward to several years later... and hold on to your seats. God breathed lots of life into our construction company. We grew and we grew fast. We were able to build our 'dream home' right on the water, which was where Clyde wanted to be. Life was good. Kids were thriving, the business was booming, and our marriage seemed to be going strong. We enjoyed many fun moments in this gorgeous home that we had designed and built together. I absolutely loved hosting people, and would have themed parties to bring people together and share the blessings that God had given us.

Our home sat towards the back of a 3.5-acre lot, close to the lake, with 7 bedrooms and 6.5 bathrooms. We thought of everything when we designed it: oversized front door, spacious living room with built-ins, fireplaces, chef's kitchen with an 11' island, butler's pantry, sunroom, private gym, in-law suite, gaming room, theater room, craft room, and a basement built for entertainment. Our backyard was a dream. We custom-built a large pool with an infinity edge, a tanning ledge, a hot tub, a slide, and a huge grotto (big enough for a group of people). It was all perfectly secured with a wrought iron gated fence.

It was a sunny September day; a 'family friend' and his husband came over for a little day-drinking and pool action - my favorite vibe. That day was special because Clyde didn't work and was able to enjoy the day with the family. It was fun and fireball for everyone. So, after the grilling was done and the sun set, I got the kids ready for bed, made sure they were snuggled in tight, and I fell asleep.

Again, my angel gave me a nudge at about 10:36 pm. The house was completely silent. The music was off. All I could hear was the waterfall from our grotto at the backyard. Where was everyone? I picked up my phone and read the text my daughter had sent to me saying, 'Mom, I think you need to get Clyde; he's acting crazy'. I took a stroll through the house, and noticed nothing. That was odd. I peeked out the front and our vehicles were in the driveway. I checked the dog cage and the dogs were sound asleep. I decided to check if anyone was out at the back. I could feel the butterflies knotting up in my stomach at this point. As I walked across the pool deck, my body felt empty and I don't even think I was breathing at the point I got closer to the grotto. I walked in, and there they were: Clyde standing up on the grotto seat, hands above his head, holding onto the ceiling, and our family friend going down on him. WTH! I screamed!

I ran back into the house, locked all the doors, and turned the pool waterfall off. My body was shaking and I couldn't breathe. I heard the garage door open and Clyde made his way into the house (I knew that was going to happen). We met face-to-face in the mudroom and, if you can believe it, Clyde started screaming at me. I remember him yelling that we were going to split up, I would be nothing without him, and that we didn't have enough sex (random). He also told me that our family friend was trying to prove that he could give 'better head' than me (The hell?). I didn't even know what to do with that information, but I made him leave the house that night. I had a lot to process.

He came back home the next morning and asked to have a talk, in the bedroom. It was the first time he was able to have a 'civil conversation' with me behind closed doors. Usually, it was in the open and in front of the kids (which drove me insane). I remember that he asked me for forgiveness, one of the very few times he did. He explained that my brother was pressuring him to do it, and that he was so drunk that he wasn't making rational decisions. He said he was ashamed of himself and that he wanted us to move past it. So, I told myself that I would forgive and TRY to forget this one (initiate punch in the gut).

A few days passed, and I could not stop thinking about what happened. I got out of bed at 3:23 am one morning, sat on the couch, and stared out the window. The cameras (duh, Monaca)! I pulled up our camera history to see what happened that night, and there it was. I could see the two of them sitting on the stairs in the pool. They were very close to each other, but I couldn't make out what they were doing. Then I saw Clyde get out of the pool and walk towards our garage; he was gone for 4 minutes. Then I saw him walk back to the pool, cigarette in hand, and motioned our family friend to go to the grotto. They proceeded to the grotto. 45 minutes passed and then you could see me walking around the pool deck in my pajamas. I walked into the grotto, then you could see me running out and back into the house. A couple minutes later, Clyde came out of the grotto, then our family friend. It wasn't until a couple of years later that my daughter finally told me what she saw that night. She saw Clyde kissing him, repeatedly.

That was the last time I would step foot in our grotto. Clyde had ruined any excitement I had of our 'dream home'.

RED FLAG

Two months later, Clyde tattooed my face on his arm.

RED FLAG

Again, I agreed to forgive and try to forget. 15 months passed and I managed to move past that night. It was Christmas; my favorite time of year. In the months leading up to the holiday, Clyde would mention wanting a golf simulator. It was a pastime that he enjoyed, and I thought it would be a great 'outlet' for him. His present that year was a $20K Golf Simulator. My present was some lingerie and a love letter:

#1 T-Shirt Girl,

Buckle up and cross your fingers, let's hope this letter makes sense. I have not written you a letter in a long time, and for that, I apologize. I just wanted to tell you what you mean to me and how much I love you. You're by far the most compassionate, kind, and giving person I have ever known. You continue to impress me with your fearlessness and faith. Your intelligence is undeniable. The love and bond you share with the kids is admirable. I almost believe you love to a fault, if that's possible. I love watching you continue to grow daily with all the new adventures that have been started recently.

I would be absolutely lost without you; you truly are the glue that holds our lives together. I know I have screwed up more than once and for that, our relationship has never been the same. I miss it, I miss us, I miss you! I sincerely apologize for the hell and pain I have caused and put you through. I am forever grateful for you finding some good in me and making it work.

Honey, I want us, need us, have to have us. Yes, I miss lots of things. I miss your laugh with me, I miss the sparkle in your eyes when you look at me, I miss flirting, I miss dates, I miss holding you, I miss our back massages, I miss waking up and watching you get ready in front of me, I miss touching you, I miss coming on to you, I miss our wild

54

nights, I miss grabbing your butt. I miss making love to you, I miss fucking you, I miss you being sweet, I miss you being dirty, I miss our trips away together, I miss lunch dates with you, I miss rubbing your legs after leg day, I miss kissing you, I miss you getting dressed up to go out to eat with me, I miss you getting dressed up for me when we get home after drinks.

That is just a fraction of what I love and miss about you. My point in writing this is to let you know how madly in love with you I am and how much I need you; it's also going to be considered a gift after I add the last paragraph. I need you to love me, I need you to want me, I need you to be in love with me, I need us back; we are on the verge of taking our professional life to another level. I want to feel whole again with the love of my life. I'm ready to get us back to our cute selves where everyone is an ornament. I long to see your heart and eyes light up again for me.

I know you really wanted to get your little mommy makeover. So, FUCK IT, BOOK IT! Let's get you recovered by summer. I still hate the idea, and do not believe that you need it, but you're very passionate about it. I can hear the excitement when you talk about it. I love you so much. If that's what you really want, I will be happy to take care of you. I'm sorry I have voiced my dismay in the past. I should have just sucked it up and let you do it.

I love you, my bride. I will continue to try my hardest, and pray every day that we get better. I cannot wait to see the new Monaca after surgery.

Love,

Clyde

After I read this letter, I was certain things were going to get better. Let's fast forward to a month and a half, and let's be in the moment when I had forgiven him again, and was trying my hardest to 'forget what happened and be the best wife I could be, so that we could be "our cute selves" again'. At this point, our construction company had expanded to other states. Clyde traveled the majority of the time, but I stayed local to take care of the kids and run the office, and I eventually even got my 'mommy makeover'.

Coming out of Covid, our construction company started taking a shift. Clyde found an opportunity for us to start contracting with a company that 'flipped houses.' We weren't excited about getting back into residential work, but we proceeded anyway. This new venture required travel, and lots of it. Clyde and the employees began traveling out of town, anywhere from 2 to 16 hours away from home.

After a few weeks stint of traveling, Clyde came home, and we had the opportunity to head out for date night. The kids were old enough to stay home, so we headed to dinner. It was a very lovely evening. On our way back to the house, we decided to stop at our neighborhood clubhouse and have a drink with some friends we hadn't seen in a while. I ordered some to-go food for the kids, and we finished our drinks. I saw that he was having a great time, and I knew that he had been out of town for a while and was 'working his little heart out.' So, I told him that I would take the food home to the kids, and he could stay and hang out.

Again, I got the kids ready for bed, made sure they were snuggled in tight, and then I fell asleep in the process. My beautiful angel nudged me at 11:37 pm. Romeo wasn't home; the clubhouse closed at 10:00 pm. Oh shit! Here we go again. I grabbed a jacket and drove my ass up to the clubhouse to find no cars in the parking lot, and an empty building. I took a stroll through the clubhouse and there wasn't a soul to be found. So, I got back in my truck and pulled up my Life360 (zoomed in, of course). It seemed like Clyde was in the back corner of the parking lot, by the dumpsters. I started to feel those nervous butterflies at this point.

As I pulled towards the back lot, I saw a bright red pair of underwear moving back and forth towards the driver's seat of a car I wasn't familiar with. I could see everything because it all happened under the streetlamp (I guess they weren't trying to hide anything. IDK). As I was pulling up, Clyde looked over his shoulder and we made eye contact. The gut-wrenching part is that he turned back and kept going! My God. I somehow threw my truck in park, grabbed my phone, held the camera button down long enough for that to pull up, swung my door open, and walked right up to the happy couple (all while taking multiple photos). As Clyde backed up, I saw the girl who was sitting at the bar when I had left earlier (no clue who she was by the way), naked from the waist down. No words were exchanged, and there was a small moment of silence. I took one look at Clyde, then back at this chick sitting in the car, and I just started punching. Lord help me, I didn't realize I had that in me, but I beat the shit out of her. My angle wasn't enough to get a good blow, so I pulled her out of the car onto the ground (by her hair, of course). Clyde grabbed me when he saw my foot swing back, before it contacted her stomach. Thank goodness for that, because I was not trying to be 'that girl.'

The struggle continued. The girl kept crying, "You're married? You're married?" I was like, "Yes bitch! He's married with 4 kids. Go home!" Clyde had grabbed my phone and was deleting the pictures. He and I 'tussled' for a while, then I managed to get in my truck and speed home. I was numb at this point, and just hopped into bed. I pulled my phone out and recovered the pictures, making sure I emailed them to myself, so that I would have evidence if I ever needed it.

Clyde kept calling me that night, yelling and screaming at me; he adamantly stated that we hash it out right then and there. He told me that he wasn't having sex with her. Okay, Clinton! Even after I saw them with my own two eyes, he tried to convince me that he didn't do it. I was beside myself. If that isn't gaslighting at its finest...

You know, I spent so much time trying to forget that night, yet it played repeatedly in my head. I would wake up at 2 or 3 in the morning and replay it over and over in my head. And per my norm, I forgave him and tried to move on.

EFFING RED FLAGS

Feeling Superior

An enduring and persistent sense of grandiosity, superiority, low empathy, and a profound need for attention and praise.

Lack of Empathy

The inability to take on another's perspective, to understand, feel, and possibly share and respond to their experience.

Gaslighting

Manipulating someone into questioning their own perception of reality. The expression, which derives from the title of the 1944 film, Gaslight, became popular in the mid-2010's. Merriam-Webster cites deception of one's memory, perception of reality, or mental stability.

Blame-Shifting

Blaming others. This can lead to the "kick the dog" effect where individuals in a hierarchy blame their immediate subordinate, and this trickles down a hierarchy until the lowest rung (the 'dog').

A common blame-shifting tactic is deflection. Deflection allows a narcissist to move the focus away from their bad behaviors and redirect the blame to something you may have said or done that is irrelevant, to confuse you, make you feel bad about yourself, and excuse themselves from having to take responsibility for their bad behavior.

The opportunity for us to work in Florida came up, and Clyde jumped on it. He moved down, along with the employees and most of the equipment. I had to trust him in Florida or else I would go crazy. Would he cheat again? How would I even know?

During his stay, I noticed another shift. He decided he was going to start a new company while down in Florida. That's interesting. I wasn't crazy about the idea at all, nor had I been crazy about the 'new opportunity' that we had been pursuing over the past year. It all felt so off.

In my continued pursuit to be the perfect wife, I helped him open his company, thinking I would be involved in the operations, just like we have always done. Instead, Clyde started taking jobs that I knew nothing about. He opened bank accounts without adding me, and eventually, I knew nothing that was going on. Whenever I called or texted him, I would get the cold shoulder, or he would get upset with me for asking questions. My gut was telling me this was his exit plan. However, he continually reassured me that it wasn't.

Narcissistic Hibernation

An intense emotional reaction experienced by a narcissistic person when they sense a setback. It can lead to withdrawal or vindictive behaviors, but it could also lead to depression and withdrawal.

About a year and a half before our separation, I had a weak moment that started from some innocent flirting with another man, 'Dwayne,' whom I knew socially. It happened while Clyde was working and living out of state. Dwayne and I began texting each other; we talked about fitness, meal prepping, and cardio subjects that we had in common and that we were passionate about. The conversations slowly turned into us sending pictures to each other to show our 'results.' Well, as you can imagine, that turned into more than it should have. We ended up sending inappropriate pictures to each other. Was I lonely? Yes, but that was no excuse.

The following morning, I got a phone call from Clyde, and he asked me, "Do anything fun last night?" Confused, I said no. He then sent me one of the inappropriate pictures that Dwayne and I had shared with each other. My immediate question was, "How did you get that picture?" I quickly realized that Clyde had logged into my Apple account and was watching what I was doing. How did he know my password? I guess he had been 'stalking' my accounts for a while.

I lied to Clyde that day and told him that Dwayne and I didn't do anything inappropriate. With him being out of town, I was able to hang up the phone and not have to answer his questions. I didn't hear from him for most of the day. That evening, I was relaxing in the bedroom when suddenly, my bedroom door swung open, and it was Clyde. He had flown up from Florida unannounced and unexpectedly. He had that 'look' on his face; that blind rage look. He snatched my phone out of my hand, headed into the living room, and started going through it. I hopped out of bed and tried to get my phone back from him. I was pissed and felt like I had no control. He pushed me away and about that time, our son walked downstairs from hearing the yelling. My heart was pounding at this point. Unfortunately, that was when I had to look at our son and tell him to call 911. Clyde stopped after that. I grabbed my phone back and locked myself in the bedroom. Like clockwork, he made his way into the bedroom and continued to scream at me. I ended up having to call 911 that night, and Clyde left the house.

Eventually, I told Clyde the truth. I was completely ashamed of myself for having a weak moment, letting my guard down, and having an inappropriate exchange. I immediately stopped talking to Dwayne. However, Clyde called Dwayne in an attempt to fact-check me. He also had the audacity to ask Dwayne if he was interested in having a threesome. What?

RED FLAG

Clyde headed back to Florida and things started going back to the way they were. It was a normal morning for me; I had just gotten back from the gym after getting the kids off to school. This was a few weeks after the 'Dwayne incident.' I grabbed my laptop to answer some emails before I hopped in the shower. I sat down in my bedroom, worked for about 45 minutes, then closed my laptop and headed to the bathroom to take a shower. After turning the water on, I proceeded to the closet to get undressed. When I walked in, my heart exploded when I saw Clyde sitting on the aisle in the middle of our closet. He didn't flinch and just sat there and stared. I don't remember exactly what I said, but it was along the lines of "Holy shit! What the hell! You scared the shit out of me." He got upset with me because I didn't act happy to see him. Instead, I felt like it was creepy.

Shortly after that, he told me that he wanted to move back to Virginia and work on our marriage. He went as far as telling me that he wanted to have another baby and wanted to start going to church with me. I remember that day like it was yesterday. I came home from work one afternoon and he asked me to sit on his lap. He looked me dead in the eyes and told me that he knew we needed to have God in our marriage and that he wanted us to start attending church again. Long story short, we didn't have another baby and we never went to church together after that conversation.

Breadcrumbing

A colloquial term used to characterize the practice of sporadically feigning interest in another person in order to keep them interested, despite a true lack of investment in the relationship. It is also called Hansel and Grettelling. It is regarded as a type of manipulation and can be either deliberate or unintentional.

Hoover Maneuver

A technique used to regain control. Coined after a popular vacuum cleaner, it refers to the fact that the abusers attempt to "suck up" the happiness of others to fuel their narcissistic impulses.

Hoovering, sometimes called "narcissistic hoovering," is a manipulative tactic used to lure or suck a person back into a relationship they're withdrawing or stepping away from. It's a way of reasserting power and control and perpetuating a cycle of abuse.

Clyde ended up moving back to Virginia, and we continued to work on our relationship and growing the business. We desired to build another house, so we decided to put our house on the market. We went as far as picking out new house plans and making a 'wish list'. Clyde started looking at lots for us to build our 'forever home'. It was exciting.

At the same time, we began another business. Clyde and a couple of his friends wanted to partner and approached me with the idea. It all sounded wonderful, and against my better judgment, we partnered with them and began a new company. We put everything we had into it. Just like our construction company, Clyde would run the operations side of the business and I would run the administrative side of things. This was when we were at our strongest; we were a power couple. The new business picked up very quickly and things were rolling. Life was good.

Even better, we had a couple that was interested in buying our house. They gave us an offer (a low-ball offer, but it was an offer), and we started negotiating. At the beginning of the negotiations, Clyde was not interested in settling for anything less than what we had paid for the house. This went on for a few weeks. By the end of the negotiations, Clyde just wanted to get rid of the house. We ended up accepting only 64% of our asking price. WTH! Why the sudden change and why was he in such a hurry?

'*****'

Chapter 6:

Don't Reshuffle the Deck and End Up with a Joker

It was an afternoon phone call on the day after we signed a contract to sell our home; I was in my office at work. The voice on the other end said, "I'm not happy; we need to separate". I hung up the call, continued working, and brushed his comment off. I truly believed he was pulling my chain. After work, I drove past a piece of property that we had been looking at to build our new house, and continued home. I noticed that he left the house before I got home. So, I did what I always did: fix dinner and hang out with the kids. As the night continued, his text messages were delayed and very short. I realized quickly that he was serious.

We had a house showing scheduled for the next day. It was for a house that we would move into after we closed; we had booked it the week before. It was the most awkward feeling walking through this house. I didn't know what to think. Clyde made it clear that he would not be moving into a house with me, but he would help me find a house for me and the kids.

Immediately, he stopped saying "I love you", wearing his wedding ring, sleeping with me, working... he stopped everything. I didn't understand how he could cut everything off cold turkey like that.

I was done trying to fight for our marriage, and all my hopes were gone, so my attitude was "I'll give him his separation." And I did just that. Just like any other 'transaction' in our relationship, I served up his separation on a silver platter. Monaca handled everything: the lawyer, the separation of assets, separating the businesses, packing the house... You name it; I took care of it. Clyde stopped showing up at work, so I was taking care of all aspects of the businesses. I did not miss a day of work. I was on autopilot, and in shock.

A month passed and we still hadn't closed on our house. Clyde and I stayed in separate rooms of the house and did not interact much at all. He would come home at 2 or 3 o'clock in the morning and go straight to his room. He kept his door locked all the time. I noticed that he would smoke cigarettes on the back deck— something that he had never done before, but was now doing openly. I would see Dr. Pepper bottles stuffed with cigarette butts, as if he was chain smoking. There were several nights when I would hear him talking on the phone, but I stayed to myself. In the mornings, I would get the kids on the bus and leave for work. We literally just crossed paths. When I asked him what he was doing until the late hours, his only comments to me were that he was "working on quotes" and "installing cameras" (to this day, those cameras are still in a box). The situation was awkward, especially since there was no work coming in through the construction company.

Nothing made sense. Everything had been going fine; we had plans to sell our house and build a new one. The new house plans were even picked out. We had a family cruise planned; we were planning a trip to Europe and we had scheduled family pictures to be taken. I didn't understand. I remember asking him if there was someone else, because that would make it make sense. He continuously reassured me that there was nobody else.

There were several nights that I remember feeling the need to just lay with him. I knew it wouldn't change anything, but I needed to feel him next to me. I learned later that this was the 'trauma bond' that had developed.

Finally, I listened to my instincts. I decided to check the phone records and see if anything would jump out at me. There was a number I didn't recognize, and it was a number that he was calling and receiving calls from every day, and at all hours of the day and night. The conversations were anywhere from 2 minutes to 2 hours. Who was this? I called Clyde and gave him the chance to confess, but he still denied that he was talking to someone else. Even though I had concrete proof that he was talking to someone, he still denied it. Who was this?

I was going to find out. I called the number. A woman's voice answered, and my first question was, "Hi, who is this?" She replied, "This is Bonnie."

"This is Monaca Vanderpool."

"Oh hey!" Bonnie replied.

"Do we know each other?" (With a caddy confusion on my face).

She responded and explained the connection (I didn't know her, but she knew who I was). She actually referred to me as "Clyde's wife".

I responded with, "Well, I was calling to see why you have been talking to my husband so much lately, but I've got all the information I need." Then I hung up.

There were those butterflies again.

Immediately, I called Clyde, told him I knew that it was Bonnie, and that this would change everything. There was a long pause, and his response was "We are only friends." I hung up.

A flood of emotions came over me at that moment, one of them being anger. I was beyond pissed and I 'proceeded accordingly.' I knew that it was time to make things about me and the kids. I also knew it was time to find out a little more about Bonnie. I started on social media and saw that she was married (classy). I was going to find out where her husband worked and give him a call.

I immediately reached out to Bonnie's husband, Roy, at work that day. I introduced myself and apologized that we had to meet on these terms, but I had some phone records that he may be interested in. Roy mentioned that he suspected there was another man. He continued to explain that he had moved out of the house a few days before (which was a few weeks after Bonnie & Clyde met), and that they were splitting up (Bonnie had a pattern of venturing out of her marriage, but that's not my story to tell). While we were on the phone, he sent me a screenshot of a man who appeared to be changing locks and ring cameras at Roy and Bonnie's house. I peeked at the picture and it was Clyde. We continued to chat and compare stories, even after that conversation. Since then, Roy and I have become great friends and consider ourselves 'Assistant Private Investigators'. We've learned a lot about keeping 'receipts', communication, and tracking devices.

The next 6 weeks were like living in hell. He continued to stay out until 2 or 3 o'clock in the morning, sometimes turning off his headlights while coming down the driveway. I guess he did this in hopes that the cameras wouldn't pick him up. I remember a particular Saturday morning when he left the house early to take Bonnie to a college football game (he wasn't a sports fan, by the way). He gave our son a kiss before he left. I started packing up the house that day—one of many days that I packed with absolutely no help from him. He did manage to pack his clothes up and stack the boxes in the corner of my bedroom – I got to look at those boxes every night.

There was another night when our son was extremely sick and I asked Clyde to bring home Pedialyte, ginger ale, and saltine crackers. I texted him numerous times because he wouldn't pick up the phone when I called. He never came home that night. Instead, he took her to a Candlelight Concert. What a romantic.

I found it very odd that he started to have sex with me again. The first time, it was about 3 o'clock in the morning (he had just gotten home) and he came into my bedroom and asked me to come to his room. He closed the door and started kissing me. One thing led to another and we started having sex. His comment after was, "This doesn't change anything." I thought to myself, "What an asshole." After that night, he wanted to have sex with me almost every time he saw me. He would send me pictures of his genitals whenever I was at work and ask me to meet him in his office. When I got to work on the day after his Candlelight Concert, he asked me to come into his office and ride him. If I ever told him, "No," his comment would be, 'This will be the last time I ask.' I was appalled when he approached me, wanting me to 'teach Bonnie how to please him.' WTH, did he really just ask me that?

I started becoming uncomfortable when he began to force himself on me. He would not take "No" for an answer. One afternoon at the office, I was walking down the hall and he came up behind me, grabbed my hands and placed them over my head, threw me up against the wall, and started kissing me and feeling up my shirt. I kept telling him to stop, but instead, he pulled me into his office and had sex with me.

Since the day he asked me for a separation, I never missed a day of work. Our employees knew the situation and I wanted them to have the security of knowing that nothing would happen to their employment. It was extremely difficult to keep a smile on my face, but I managed to do it. There was a day that I called my office staff and told them that I couldn't come in. They could sense that something was off, and something was. The night before, Clyde had forced himself on me while making comments like, "If you would have been a dirty slut for me, we would still be together". He then ejaculated on my face. I felt so disgusted the next day; I couldn't bring myself to get dressed and go to work.

Trauma Bond

Emotional bonds that arise from a cyclical pattern of abuse. A trauma bond occurs in an abusive relationship, wherein the victim forms an emotional bond with the perpetrator.

Some long-term impacts of trauma bonding include remaining in abusive relationships, adverse mental health outcomes like low self-esteem, negative self-image, an increased likelihood of depression and bipolar disorder, and perpetuating a generational cycle of abuse. Many abuse victims who experience trauma bonding return to the abusive relationship.

Pathological Lying

A chronic behavior characterized by the habitual or compulsive tendency to lie. It involves a pervasive pattern of intentionally making false statements with the aim of deceiving others, sometimes without a clear or apparent reason. Individuals who engage in pathological lying often claim to be unaware of the motivations behind their lies.

The stories are presented in a way in which the liar is portrayed in a favorable manner. The liar 'decorates their own person' by telling stories that present them as the hero or the victim.

Gaslighting

Manipulating someone into questioning their own perception of reality. The expression, which derives from the title of the 1944 film Gaslight, became popular in the mid-2010's. Merriam-Webster cites deception of one's memory, perception of reality, or mental stability.

Coercion

Involves compelling a party to act in an involuntary manner by the use of threats, including threats to use force against that party. It involves a set of forceful actions which violate the free will of an individual in order to induce a desired response. These actions may include extortion, blackmail, or even torture and sexual assault.

Coercion used as leverage may force victims to act in a way contrary to their own interests. Coercion can involve psychological abuse.

Sexual Coercion is unwanted sexual penetration after pressure in a non-physical way. 27.2% of women and 11.7% of men experience unwanted sexual contact.

Marital Rape or Spousal Rape

The act of sexual intercourse with one's spouse without the spouse's consent. The lack of consent is the essential element and doesn't always involve physical violence. Marital rape is considered a form of domestic violence and sexual abuse.

Marital rape is illegal in all fifty states. In most states, marital and non-marital rape are treated equally. Do your research and know the laws. Marital rape is NOT okay!

Nearly 1 in 5 women (18.3%) and 1 in 71 men (1.4%) have been raped in their lifetime. Nearly 1 in 10 women (9.4%) in the US have been raped by an intimate partner in their lifetime.

THIS.IS.NOT.OK!!

Chapter 7:

Salt in the Wound

Thank goodness that our house finally closed; it felt like the longest 2 months of my life. Thankfully, I took the time in those 8 weeks to pack what I could. Although Clyde had told me he was going to help me move into my new house, I ended up hiring a moving company to move my stuff. I had scheduled the movers to come the day after Thanksgiving. This would allow me and the kids to sit down and enjoy our Thanksgiving meal together. I ordered a ready-to-go meal from Cracker Barrel, and even ordered extra so that Clyde could have a nice meal, but he never touched it. I'm sure he was full from his Friendsgiving meal he ate with Bonnie and her crew.

At this point, I was getting very irritated by Clyde's actions. He kept wanting to have sex and even wanted me to call him if I ever hooked up with anyone because he wanted to come over afterwards with a friend to continue with a threesome (and to make sure I didn't shower). My goodness, what is up with the threesomes?

Clyde had started dropping hints that he was going to be taking a trip to Las Vegas. I didn't pay too much attention to it because it was during my weekend with our son. The night before he was supposedly leaving, he sent me a text saying, "Do you want to cum?" I replied, "No!" He sent me two more texts after that, asking the same thing. I repeatedly replied "No!" He ended up at Bonnie's house and spent the night with her instead. The next day at work, an employee of the construction company (which I had signed over to Clyde), came into my office asking about his paycheck. I was no longer involved with that company, but the employees were like family to me, and I would do anything to make sure they were taken care of. So, I texted Clyde to ask him about their paychecks. His response was, "I will call you when I land." I assumed he was on his flight to Vegas. I never heard from him for the rest of the day, or throughout the weekend. To be honest, I didn't mind. But it was interesting that I later saw a Snapchat picture of him, Bonnie, and the kids skiing in West Virginia. Roy also got a message from his kid that he was with them, skiing. It was so interesting how information just fell on my lap. The following Monday, he stopped by the office (rare moment), and his truck was covered in the salt from the roads. So, why he told me he was going to Vegas was beyond me.

The lies were beginning to add up; they were constant. While going through my calendar, looking at dates and conversations, and comparing notes with Roy, I noticed that nothing added up. He was never where he said he was.

We agreed to split the proceeds from the house evenly. We were fortunate enough to pay for our house, as we were building and we didn't carry a mortgage. So, when the house closed, we both got a substantial amount of money. Thankfully, I was able to buy a home for me and the kids.

Clyde took a different approach. He chose to rent a house (2 ½ blocks away from Bonnie) and use the rest for clothes, shoes, and trips that he had been 'so deprived of' during our marriage. Every time I saw him, he was dressed to the nines, losing weight, and rocking Tiffany cologne. A few days before Christmas, he came to my office and shared that he had 2 ski trips coming up. Mind you, he had never skied a day in his life. He told me that these trips were with 'Bonnie and a group of friends'. At this point, I wasn't even upset about him going on trips with her; I just didn't like that he didn't consider asking me to take our son during his scheduled days during these trips. Just like it was when we were together, he assumed that the world revolved around him.

Still convincing me that they were 'just friends', they were holding hands and kissing at the airport before departing for their ski trip to Montana.

About a year before the separation, Clyde and I had started looking at 'Airbnb's. We had a plan to start purchasing in Nashville, Scottsdale, Florida, and at a beach somewhere. My dream was to turn them into Bachelorette-Themed 'Airbnb's." I thought it would be a great way to begin our retirement plan, bring in some 'mailbox money,' and offer me something fun and enjoyable to run. Well, it turned out that Clyde was supposedly buying up land and properties in all these cities. It was like he was taking my dream and moving forward with it, but without me. What a punch in the gut. He also informed me that he was purchasing a piece of land and would start building his dream home.

Nice, Clyde!

Separating the businesses was an absolute nightmare. It felt like an eternity, and just when I thought we were making progress, another 'issue' would come up that we had to deal with. This made it very difficult to work with Clyde. We both wanted everything to be over, and neither of us wanted to pay for the other person's stuff. So, determining who owned what, and who would get what was exhausting.

Clyde became difficult to deal with. Our phone conversations became very toxic, and our text messaging was no better.

Somewhere along the way, he 'unfriended' me on social media after updating his profile picture to a picture of him on the slopes.

It was a Thursday, and I was headed to a meeting. I was cruising down the highway, listening to music, sipping on a cup of coffee, and I heard a car honking repeatedly. I looked to my left and there was Clyde, waving his hands around dramatically, flipping me off, and then speeding past me. I took a sip of my coffee and continued to my meeting. It was stuff like this that I had to deal with.

_____

"This is why we can't have nice things.
Because you break them, I had to take them away."
                                                    Taylor Swift

_____

Epilogue:

A Queen Busy with Her Kingdom

As time passed, my heart became very closed off to anything that involved Clyde. I couldn't stand all the lying, and frankly, the sight of him made me sick. I ended up having to block him on all social media platforms, as well as my phone, which was unfortunate because we needed to communicate. If it was work-related, I would email him and copy my lawyer. If it was personal, I used a co-parenting app to message him, as well as created a calendar for anything related to our son. Like clockwork, he was still able to take 'jabs' at me on those platforms. He ended all his emails with, "Have a blessed day! We will pray for you," or "Cheers!" It was annoying, but I learned to ignore all the cattiness.

I learned a technique called 'grey rocking'. I wish I had known about it years ago; it became a method I used to protect my peace. It diverts a toxic person's behavior by acting as unresponsive as possible when you're interacting with them. I avoided making eye contact and I didn't show emotions during our conversations. He couldn't fight against air.

My new home feels different. There is love and laughter, and we no longer have to walk on eggshells. We can be ourselves. I have even noticed that I spend more time with the kids. We eat meals together, watch movies, and play games. My favorite is when they come into my room and just hang out. We don't have to say any words, but we're in each other's presence.

We are thriving. I'm in a season of being completely devoted to God.

"I know what it is to have little, and I know what it is to have plenty. In any and all circumstances I have learned the secret of being happy"
Philippians 4:12

I spent a while trying to figure out what was God's purpose for me after all of this. I had spent so many years giving everything I had to a relationship that would end. I had set myself up for financial dependency on someone who had left me, cold turkey. I refused to think I was 'stuck'. I serve a God who orders my every step, and who will be with me and take care of me always. He works all things out for the good and the 'crushing' that I had been going through was only preparing me for what He has for me.

"The steps of a good man are ordered by the Lord, and he delights in his ways."
Psalm 37:23

"She confidently trusts the Lord to take care of her."
Psalm 112:7

"All things work together for good to those who love God, who have been called according to his purpose."

I woke up one morning, and God reminded me to "rejoice in my sufferings, knowing that suffering produces endurance, and endurance produces character, and character produces hope, and hope does not put me to shame, because God's love has been poured into my heart through the Holy Spirit who has been given to me." (Romans 5:3-5) God wants to turn our pain into purpose and He is always working for our good.

So, at the beginning of 2024, I began the Glitch Mob Podcast, a platform to talk about these topics openly, to educate others, and to help those who are in similar situations-not just toxic relationships and narcissism, but mental health, self-care, self-love, financial independence, co-parenting, single parenting, and much more. There is beauty in breaking down these topics, and I want to build a community where we can make a difference and change these 'glitches' that have crept their way into our lives.

You are not a victim for sharing your story.
You are a survivor setting the world on fire with your truth.
You never know who needs your light, your warmth, and raging courage.

-Alex Elle

ᵗ*******ᵗ

If you are in a relationship where your well-being is threatened in any way – emotionally, psychologically, or physically – then it is toxic. If a relationship leaves you feeling unsupported, misunderstood, demeaned, or attacked, then it is toxic. If you are in a toxic relationship, you are allowed to leave!

I stayed in a toxic relationship for 13 years and, along the way, there were several times that I knew deep down that I should have left, but I didn't. I was also unaware of the signs and 'red flags' that I should have paid attention to. There were several red flags and traits to be aware of and I'm only sharing those that pertain to my story. My prayer is that this book will help others who have experienced similar things. Even if I help one person, this is all worth it.

Monaca's Glossary

Affairs

When you are in a committed relationship (i.e. marriage), and you go outside of that to find comfort or pleasure, you are having an affair. Whether it's emotional, physical, or sexual, it is cheating and is a betrayal of trust, especially if you are having to hide the affair. Sadly, trust can take years to build, but seconds to break.

If your partner is secretly communicating with 'a friend', prioritizing that friend over you, not communicating when they are hanging out, or getting defensive when you share feelings about their friend, then they are having an emotional affair. Run!

"But a man who commits adultery has no sense;
whoever does so destroys himself."

Proverbs 6:32

Unfortunately, Clyde had numerous affairs: emotional, physical, and sexual. Cheating sucks! It was the biggest 'middle finger' at my ability to open my heart and trust, and it screamed volumes about his relationship with himself. It was hurtful, deceitful, and gross. I didn't understand his behavior because it never crossed my mind to act in the same way. I don't have a specific reason why I stayed. Perhaps it was because it was easier for me to stay, or because I didn't want another failed marriage, or maybe because part of me felt like I wasn't being the wife I should have been. All I know is that I loved Clyde and I wanted to be with him. We shared life events, children, memories, and special moments together.

While I've certainly not arrived yet, I've gained more healing than I ever thought possible.

Chapter 5

Blame-shifting

Blaming others leads to the "kick the dog" effect where individuals in a hierarchy blame their immediate subordinate, and this trickles down the hierarchy until the lowest rung (the 'dog').

A common blame-shifting tactic is deflection. Deflection allows a narcissist to move the focus away from their bad behaviors and redirect the blame to something you may have said or done that is irrelevant, to confuse you, make you feel bad about yourself, and excuse themselves from having to take responsibility for their bad behavior.

When a narcissist gets caught, they will shift the blame to you, to avoid focusing on their bad behavior. It is a form of gas-lighting, which is emotional abuse. They might say, "You made me do this", or "It's your fault I'm like this". They want to make you feel responsible for their negative behavior. This would leave you feeling confused.

The majority of our 'fights' shifted to something Clyde thought I did wrong. Even when I caught him in the act of cheating, he insisted on focusing the spotlight on me. It was unreal. He would also throw random comments into the conversation that had nothing to do with what we were talking about; it made no sense. This is what I call a "word salad".

You must hold on to your reality. Don't defend it because the narcissist isn't listening. You can't get lost in the blame that they tried to shift to you. In your mind, always move the spotlight to the original issue; everything else is not even relevant.

"Why do you look at the speck that is in your brother's eye, but do not notice the log that is in your own eye? Or how can you say to your brother, 'Let me take the speck out of your eye,' and behold, the log is in your own eye? You hypocrite, first take the log out of your own eye, and then you will see clearly to take the speck out of your brother's eye."

Matthew 7:3-5

Chapter 5

Breadcrumbing.

An unofficial term used to characterize the practice of sporadically feigning interest in another person in order to keep them interested, despite a true lack of investment in the relationship. This is also called Hansel and Grettelling. It is regarded as a type of manipulation and can be either deliberate or unintentional.

A narcissist will drop small 'morsels of interest' to make you feel like they're still interested. Whether it's intentional or not, breadcrumbing is a form of manipulation and is used by a narcissist to maintain control.

This was what kept me around for so long. The love-bombing, the love letters, the sweet text messages; they all gave me 'hope' that things would get better. The bottom line is that we can't live on breadcrumbs.

Chapters 4 & 6

Coercive Control

In their constant drive to be the superior one, a narcissist would like to control everyone. How annoying! At first, they try to impress you, but eventually, their own needs will always come first. This is because, for narcissists, control is the equivalent of power.

Some examples of Coercive control are:

- Monitoring your behavior (online or in person)
- Isolating you from your family or friends (or business associates)
- Controlling what you wear, eat, or do
- Controlling who you are allowed to spend time with
- Gaslighting
- Tracking you

Honestly, these are all forms of bullying and, eventually, will leave you restricted and make it hard to leave the relationship.

I'm surprised that I didn't notice the control in our first year together, especially when he was going through my social media accounts. It didn't bother me because I had nothing to hide. That was only the beginning of what would be 13 years of it. The isolation from business associates, introducing 'friends' into our bedroom, and tracking my Apple account were all signs of coercive control.

CYCLE OF NARCISSISTIC ABUSE

This is a pattern of harmful behaviors used by someone with narcissistic traits to manipulate and exploit another person. The cycle is emotionally devastating and includes the following stages:

1. Idealization or Love-Bombing
2. Devaluation
3. Discard
4. Hoovering or Re-engagement

By maneuvering through these stages, the abuser gains a sense of power and control over the victim's emotions, thoughts, and behaviors. It creates a persistent state of dependency within the victim.

Chapter 2

Devaluing

The dynamics of our relationship started to shift dramatically. The intense affection and positive attention I was getting started to lessen. It was like Clyde's perfect vision of me was no longer perfect. It started to make me feel insecure. The honeymoon was over.

There's a stage called 'devaluation'. It's when your flaws and weaknesses take center stage, and your positive qualities are completely ignored. It's like they don't see you as a 'good person' any longer. These negative feelings lead to anger & contempt. They start devaluing you when you become too difficult for them to control, or you are easily manipulated, causing them to look down upon you.

Devaluing can take many forms. They may embarrass and demean you in public, make you feel unimportant and insignificant, or even criticize you and verbally attack you. In some cases, like mine, explosive and impulsive outbursts of anger and aggression begin. Rage was an emotion that I never saw growing up. My parents were always levelheaded, and I never remember them raising their voices. This was new to me, and I didn't know how to deal with it (although nobody should ever have to 'deal' with it).

Some people will never value who we are, no matter how good we become. Even Jesus was devalued. Look at how he was taken for granted in Matthew 11. When he had finished instructing his twelve disciples, he went on to teach and preach in their cities, and they didn't believe in him. Even after all the miracles, (he raised people from the dead and healed the sick), people still rejected him.

How did Jesus respond? He basically moved on; He moved on to those who would value him. He didn't become hardened or close himself off from all people, even after being bluntly disrespected. Isn't that our natural temptation to allow life circumstances to allow us to become hardened? Not Jesus. He ignored them and focused on His mission.

> *"Come to me, all you who are weary and burdened, and I will give you rest. Take my yoke upon you and learn from me; for I am gentle and humble in heart, and you will find rest for your souls. For my yoke is easy and my burden is light."*
>
> *Matthew 11: 28-30*

Gentle and Humble. Jesus could have become prideful and selfish by saving his gifts for only himself, but instead, he invited others in who would value him and what he had to offer. This is an example of how we are to handle those who dishonor us. Instead of becoming hardened, locking up who you are, or devaluing yourself into a woman or man of lower standards, move on like Jesus and let God handle the rest.

Protect yourself and protect your peace! Keep your heart soft and tender towards the Lord and those he has assigned to your life. They will value you for who you really are.

Chapter 5

Feeling Superior

A persistent sense of grandiosity, superiority, low empathy, and a profound need for attention and praise. I call it being arrogant and cocky; thinking you are better than someone else.

Narcissists want to get what they want, when they want it, and how they want it, even when they shouldn't. They believe that they make the rules. They have affairs because it makes them feel powerful and superior.

"Always be humble and gentle. Be patient with each other, making allowance for each other's faults because of your love."
Ephesians 4:2

"Do nothing from rivalry or conceit, but in humility count others more significant than yourselves."
Philippians 2:3

"Be humble and never think that you are better than anyone else...for dust you are and to dust you will return."
Genesis 3:19

"God opposes the proud but gives grace to the humble."
James 4:6

Or in the famous words of Tim McGraw....always stay humble and kind!

Chapter 3

Financial Dependency

Friends, women especially, do not give up your financial independence! This is something I kick myself in the butt for doing. I put myself in a position where I was dependent on Clyde for our financial stability. It put me in a position of being 'stuck' and made it difficult to leave the relationship. It was one of the reasons I stayed as long as I did.

Financial dependency and control are other tactics that narcissist use to isolate their victims. They can do this in several ways: limiting your access to money, preventing you from pursuing your career, or manipulating your financial decisions.

In my situation, I needed Clyde in the 'equation' of our business in order to make an income. But, let's not get it twisted, Clyde and I both needed each other in the equation in order for the business to be successful. When our marriage ended, it wasn't clear who would take what. We had two businesses and neither of them were industries that I wanted to be in. I ended up picking the 'path of least resistance', and even then, ended up leaving it because my heart was not in it.

Everything was in my name, and I mean everything. The businesses, the vehicles, and the assets all had my name attached to them, making me liable for more than I should have been liable for. Due to his 'history', we had no choice but to put everything in my name, and at the time, I assumed we would be together forever, so I didn't hesitate. It was a nightmare to separate and unravel everything. My biggest piece of advice is to protect yourself and hire a good lawyer and financial advisor. It will be worth it!

Chapter 5 & 6

Gaslighting

I feel like this was the word of the year in 2023. I wish I had known about gaslighting years ago, at least to be aware of it before it got out of control. Gaslighting is a repetitive set of manipulation tactics that makes you question reality. Narcissists use it to protect their ego, keep others from challenging them, and to maintain a sense of superiority over others. Talk about control!

My famous experience with gaslighting was when I would smell cigarette smoke on Clyde. I would ask him if he had been smoking, and he would deny it every time. He would always say, "What are you talking about, Monaca?" There was a moment when I questioned whether I knew what cigarette smoke smelled like. It was so stupid. Eventually, I could predict when he was going to gaslight me.

They will use 'diverting' to gaslight you. This occurs when the abuser changes the subject to avoid talking about the actual subject. Another tactic is that they will 'forget' or 'deny' that something happened. They flat-out lie to your face without showing any sign that they are doing it. Or one tactic that I experienced quite a bit, was 'trivializing'. They make your feelings and opinions seem like they are unimportant or irrelevant. Talk about thinking you're the crazy one! Finally, they'll begin to 'stonewall'. This is where they shut down and refuse to continue a conversation. They'll say something like, "This conversation is over" or "I'm not talking about this anymore". All these tactics leave you feeling small and insignificant. They make you insecure about your thoughts and feelings.

I love this scripture and it has helped me get through the moments when I was feeling confused. We don't serve a God of confusion. Ask God to give you clarity and peace, and He will do just that.

The Bible speaks strongly against behavior that leads to gaslighting. Proverbs 12 tells us that it's important to speak in a way that brings healing, not harm. It also shows us the importance of honesty. This tells me that gaslighting someone goes against God's wishes and can have serious consequences.

Chapter 1

Grandiosity

A sense of superiority, uniqueness, or invulnerability that is unrealistic and not based on personal capability. It may be expressed by exaggerated beliefs regarding one's abilities, the belief that few other people have anything in common with oneself, and that one can only be understood by a few, very special people. The personality trait of grandiosity is principally associated with narcissistic personality disorder (NPD).

1. The person exaggerates talents, capacity, and achievements in an unrealistic way.
2. The person has grandiose fantasies.
3. The person believes that they do not need other people.
4. The person over-examines and downgrades other people's projects, statements, or dreams in an unrealistic manner.
5. The person regards themself as unique or special when compared to other people.
6. The person regards themself as generally superior to other people.
7. The person behaves self-centeredly and/or self-referentially.
8. The person behaves in a boastful or pretentious way.

This is a defining characteristic of narcissism-the exaggerated feelings of superiority, entitlement, self-importance, obsessive need for admiration, and a lack of empathy toward others.

"If you want to boast, boast in the Lord"
2 Corinthians 10:17

Epilogue

Grey Rocking

It's a technique that diverts a toxic person's behavior by acting as unresponsive as possible when you're interacting with them. I avoided making eye contact and I didn't show emotions during our conversations. The idea behind this technique is that abusive people, especially those with narcissistic tendencies, enjoy getting a reaction from their victims. Refusing to give them this reaction makes interactions less rewarding for them.

Here are a few techniques:

- Giving short, noncommittal, or one-word answers.
- Keeping interactions short.
- Avoiding arguments, no matter what someone says or does to provoke it.
- Keeping personal or sensitive information private.
- Showing no emotion or vulnerability.
- Minimizing contact, such as by waiting long periods before responding to texts or leaving a call as quickly as possible.

Although this method isn't guaranteed to work, it sure did protect my peace. Clyde couldn't fight against air and after we separated, the only reason we need to communicate is our son.

Chapter 5

Hoover Maneuver

This phrase was coined after the popular vacuum cleaner, and is a technical term used by many. It refers to the fact that the abuser attempts to 'suck up' your happiness or suck you back into the toxic relationship. Abusers will 'hoover' you because they fear that you are getting away from them. Hence, they engage in tactics such as love bombing, stalking, triangulation, etc.

I would like to take a moment and emphasize that this is not a term that I coined (although it would have been ironic if I had).

Had I coined this phrase, I would have put it on a t-shirt, just saying #hoovermaneuver.

Chapter 2

Intimidation

A behavior which usually involves deterring or coercing an individual by threat of violence. This includes intentional behaviors of forcing another person to experience general discomfort such as humiliation, embarrassment, inferiority, limited freedom, etc. Intimidation is done to make the other person submissive (also known as *cowing*), to destabilize/undermine the other, to force compliance, to hide one's insecurities, to socially valorize oneself, etc.

This is another form of narcissistic abuse. It involves aggression, bullying, and manipulation. After experiencing it, you realize that your abuser is unpredictable. It causes us to 'walk on eggshells' and leaves us in a constant state of anxiety and fear. You find yourself always guessing how not to trigger them. You're damned if you do something, and you're damned if you don't. So exhausting!

Behaviors of intimidation include condescending, degrading, patronizing or disparaging remarks, rudeness, sarcasm, disrespect, etc. It comes from the Latin word *intimidate*, which means to 'make timid'.

Clyde's intimidation was so intense that I had to call 911 to protect myself on many occasions. Nothing about that was okay. There were moments when I feared my own husband and I didn't know how to get away from him.

"Wives, submit to your husbands as to the Lord."

Ephesians 5:22

My bible says to submit to my husband, but not if my husband does not submit to the Lord. When you are disrespected or abused, you should respect yourself enough not to submit to anyone who does not submit to God.

Chapter 3

Isolation

This refers to the near or complete lack of social contact by an individual. Isolating targeted victims enables a narcissist to better manipulate and control them. When it comes to their partner and children, they isolate them from the outside world, from one another, and even from their own sense of reality. They want to keep you to themselves, so that they can control you and every aspect of your life. They also want to keep your attention focused solely on them. There'd be no room for anyone else in your life.

Narcissists thrive on power and control, and will go to great lengths to maintain it. Some of the tactics they use are dictating who you can and can't spend time with, monitoring your communications and social media accounts, or controlling your finances. They want to separate you from your support system. They also want to keep your attention focused solely on them.

If you aren't aware of them isolating you, you will begin to feel like you 'need them', which makes them your 'primary provider'. Before you know it, you're developing an addictive cycle because you want to keep coming back.

I remember Clyde telling me that I would be nothing without him, and he believed that. Over the years, he slowly isolated me from my business colleagues, my friends, and even some of my family. He was keeping me all to himself. Thankfully, I am free from that now.

Chapter 5

Lack of empathy

This is the inability to take on another's perspective, to understand, feel, and possibly share and respond to their experience. This is a trait that I honestly can't wrap my head around. Being with someone who is not compassionate or sympathetic is hard—very hard. They are insensitive and unable to consider another person's feelings and experiences. A narcissist will cheat because they have little or no empathy towards their partner.

"Carry each other's burdens."
Galatians 6:2

"Therefore, as God's chosen people, holy and dearly loved, clothe yourself with compassion, kindness, humility, gentleness, and patience."
Colossians 3:12

"Be kind and compassionate to one another, forgiving each other, just as in Christ God forgave you."
Ephesians 4:32

"For you were called to freedom, brothers. Only do not use your freedom as an opportunity for the flesh, but through love serve one another."
Galatians 5:13

"Blessed are the merciful, for they will be shown mercy."
Matthew 5:7

"Love your neighbor as yourself."
Mark 12:31

The bottom line is that we are commanded to love our neighbor. Yet, we often overlook opportunities to relieve others' pain. Empathy is the key that can unlock the door to our kindness and compassion.

Chapter 1

Love Bombing

There are so many resources out there that explain the dangers of love bombing. Although, if we're being honest, it feels so good, doesn't it? I mean, who doesn't want to be showered with love, adoration, gifts, compliments, and attention? It always feels good to be someone's priority. Clyde and I wanted to be with each other 24/7. We moved in together very early on, we started saying "I love you" quickly, we showered each other with expensive gifts (I should share the story of me buying him a Ford Excursion), and it felt like it was 'too good to be true'. These were all signs of love bombing. At the time, I didn't know much about it and wasn't aware that it was happening.

There are several other signs of love bombing. If your significant other is pushing you to make commitments, creating a false version of themselves based on what you like, complimenting you excessively, or being overly possessive, then be aware that you are being love-bombed. Experiencing this can leave you incredibly conflicted. What's happening internally is increased rushes of dopamine, and all those 'feel good hormones', making you feel exhilarated. It's like a drug.

Narcissists will target someone who is strong-willed and who has talents and characteristics they admire because they believe these characteristics would make them shine too. I think it's a beautiful thing when you see a woman who is independent and strong. Unfortunately, that makes us targets.

I find it interesting that the media portrays fast-moving, extravagant, love-at-first-sight romances as being okay. I've never been into those reality shows for that reason, and it can be a breeding ground for disaster.

If someone is love-bombing you, I'm not saying they are bad or that they are considered your enemy. What I'm saying is that it's a sign that they may be dealing with emotional difficulties. There's nothing wrong with that, but acknowledge your emotions and practice healthy emotional control. Also, be aware that this can be the beginning of the cycle.

Chapter 6

Marital or Spousal Rape

This is the act of sexual intercourse with one's spouse without the spouse's consent. The lack of consent is the essential element and doesn't always involve physical violence. Marital rape is considered a form of domestic violence and sexual abuse.

First of all, rape is not about sex. Sex becomes the weapon and vehicle to accomplish the desired result, which is to overwhelm, overpower, embarrass, and humiliate another person. All NONCONSENSUAL sex is rape, whether it takes place in a marriage or not.

"Husbands, love your wives and do not be harsh with them."
Colossians 3:19

Marital rape is illegal in all fifty states. In most states, marital and non-marital rape are treated equally. Do your research and know the laws. Marital rape is NOT OKAY!

Sex is to be God-honoring, exclusive, and loving. It should happen regularly, and it should be unifying and mutually agreed upon.

> *"Do not deprive one another, except perhaps by agreement for a limited time, that you may devote yourselves to prayer; but then come together again, so that Satan may not tempt you because of your lack of self-control."*
>
> *1 Corinthians 7:5*

God knows what's up! The Bible tells us that the husband should provide satisfaction to his wife and a wife should provide sexual satisfaction to her husband. Does this mean that either of them can force themselves on the other? ABSO-EFFING-LUTELY NOT! The passage is about giving satisfaction, not demanding it.

THIS.IS.NOT.OK!!

A note to victims: if anyone has ever made sexual contact with you without your consent, please seek help. RAINN (Rape, Abuse, and Incest National Network) is always available online or you can call them.

Narcissism

This is extreme self-involvement to the degree that it makes a person ignore the needs of those around them (WebMD). While everyone may show occasional narcissistic behavior, true narcissists frequently disregard others or their feelings. They also don't understand the effect that their behavior has on other people. If a person has an excessive interest in or admiration of themselves, if they lack empathy for others, or if they believe others to be inferior, they are showing qualities of a narcissist.

"I never trust a narcissist, but they love me."
Taylor Swift (2017)

Chapter 5

Narcissistic Hibernation

This is an intense emotional reaction experienced by a narcissistic person when they sense a setback. It can lead to withdrawal or vindictive behaviors, but it could also lead to depression and withdrawal.

I honestly can't count how many times Clyde went into hibernation. He was gone for most of our relationship, either at the office 'working', or out of town. I can't speak much on it; I just know it exists. Perhaps it was a good thing for me; I was mostly at peace during those times.

Chapter 6

Pathological Lying

A chronic behavior characterized by the habitual or compulsive tendency to lie. It involves a pervasive pattern of intentionally making false statements with the aim of deceiving others, sometimes without a clear or apparent reason. Individuals who engage in pathological lying often claim to be unaware of the motivations behind their lies.

The stories are presented in a way in which the liar is portrayed in a favorable manner. The liar 'decorates their own person' by telling stories that present them as the hero or the victim.

"The Lord detests lying lips, but he delights in people who are trustworthy."

Proverbs 12:22

A pathological liar is someone who lies compulsively and without any clear benefit. Most of us have told a white lie to protect someone's feelings, or stretched the truth a bit to get out of something we didn't want to do or to avoid conflict. In any situation, lying isn't ideal. When it becomes a habit, that's the problem. A narcissist would typically start to believe their own lies. It becomes a huge web.

Over time, you lose trust and don't know what to believe. Even when they speak the truth, you second guess whether to believe them or not.

Chapter 2

Rage

This is an intense, uncontrolled anger that is an increased stage of hostile response to a perceived egregious injury or injustice. Rage is from C. 1300, meaning 'madness, insanity; a fit of frenzy; rashness, foolhardiness, intense or violent emotion, anger, wrath; fierceness in battle; violence'.

Rage can sometimes lead to a state of mind where the individuals experiencing it believe they can do, and often are capable of doing, things that may normally seem physically impossible. Those experiencing rage usually feel the effects of high adrenaline levels in the body. This increase in adrenal output raises the physical strength and endurance levels of the person and sharpens their senses, while dulling the sensation of pain. High levels of adrenaline impair memory.

A person in a state of rage may also lose much of their capacity for rational thought and reasoning, and may act, usually violently, on their impulses to the point that they may attack until they have been incapacitated, or the source of their rage has been destroyed or otherwise removed.

"A hot-tempered man stirs up strife, but he who is slow to anger quiets contention."

Proverbs 15:18

"For man's anger does not bring about the righteous life that God desires."

James 1:20

"Get rid of all bitterness, passion, and anger. No more shouting or insults, no more hateful feelings of any sort."

Ephesians 4:31

"Refrain from anger and turn from wrath; do not fret – it leads only to evil."

Psalm 37:8

Chapter 6

Sexual Coercion.

This is a form of Coercive Control. It is when a person pressures, tricks, threatens, or manipulates you into sex – which is a form of sexual assault. It is not ok! Even if you are saying 'yes', you are not freely giving your consent.

See "Marital/Spousal Rape"

'*****'

Chapter 6

Trauma Bond.

My relationship with Clyde was strengthened because I found comfort in the pain, as fucked up as that sounds. Extremely unhealthy. I developed a trauma bond because he went back and forth, from being kind and affectionate to being abusive. It built this intimacy level that made it easy to overlook, and not recognize the abuse that started to happen. I remembered the happy times and convinced myself to stay. When a relationship starts with instant attraction and irresistible chemistry, it's highly physical and sexual. Then, the relationship cycles through extreme highs and lows, you are prone to develop a 'trauma bond' with that person. It feels like an addiction that you are powerless to quit.

I was so emotionally attached to Clyde that I formed this deep attachment that developed through all the cycles of trauma/abuse followed by positive reinforcement. I had lost my sense of self. It was because of this 'trauma bond' that I had the desire to just lay with him, even after he asked me for a separation, and I knew we wouldn't be together. Thank goodness that only lasted for a short period of time.

You may have heard of "Stockholm Syndrome", a theory that tries to explain why hostages sometimes develop a psychological bond with their captors. Same concept.

Look at the Israelites after they escaped Egypt. After being freed from 430 years of bondage, after crossing the Red Sea on dry land and seeing the Egyptians drown, after being sent bread from heaven every day for 40 years, after moving towards the Promised Land, they still thought it would be better to go back to Egypt and to their slavery. That is an example of a trauma bond. They wanted to go back to what they were familiar with, the predictability of the past started looking pretty good.

Chapter 4

Triangulation.

"The man said, 'This is now bone of my bones and flesh of my flesh; she shall be called 'woman,' for she was taken out of man. That is why a man leaves his father and mother and is united to his wife, and they become one flesh."

Genesis 2:23-24

God's intention for marriage is for a man to 'leave' his parents and 'cling' to his wife. The man's duty is to forsake his parents in the sense that he transfers his loyalty from them to his wife. I love that word, 'loyalty'. Jesus repeats this principle of Matthew 19:3-9 when he says, 'they are no longer two, but one' and 'What God has joined together, man must never separate.'

In my eyes, my marriage was something sacred and I never thought it was okay to bring anyone else into it. At the same time, I struggled with knowing that my husband wanted something different, and I wasn't giving that to him. I let my guard down, as well as my values and beliefs, to make him happy. Which, in the long run, did me absolutely no good. Wake up, Monaca!

This is an interesting tactic. Triangulation is when the abuser intentionally introduces a third party into the relationship, forming a 'triangle', to remain in control. So, basically a 'threesome' you didn't agree to. It's a manipulation tool. It's not uncommon for people to unintentionally employ triangulation because conflict is difficult and uncomfortable to navigate. Narcissistic triangulation is different in that it is done purposefully and with intention. For you, it creates jealousy, a sense of competition, and insecurity.

Once you recognize and understand narcissistic triangulation, the next step is to decide if you want to change the dynamic. Avoiding or stopping it is complicated and will more than likely result in conflict. So, it's important to respond, not react to it. Being silent is the loudest way to communicate your boundaries.

Word Salad

A narcissist will throw random words and comments into the conversation that have nothing to do with what you are talking about, and it makes no sense. They do this to throw you off and distract you from the point you are trying to make. It basically leaves you feeling like you're crazy and, in some cases, leads you to completely forget what you were originally talking about.

'********'

Boundaries

Can we make this the word of the year? Seriously!

"Above all else, guard your heart, for everything you do flows from it."

Proverbs 4:23

It is so important for us to set boundaries and protect them. Emotions, thoughts, and desires flow from our hearts. So, guarding your heart is a foundational principle for establishing emotional and spiritual boundaries.

"'I have the right to do anything.' you say – but not everything is beneficial. 'I have the right to do anything' – but I will not be mastered by anything."

1 Corinthians 6:12

There is a balance between freedom and self-restraint. We have to consider the impact of our actions and avoid being controlled by anything. God is telling us to set healthy personal boundaries.

'********'

Forgiveness.

"For if you forgive other people when they sin against you, your heavenly Father will also forgive you."

Matthew 6:14

That's all the scripture I need to read to know that I need to forgive anyone who has sinned against me, including Clyde. Now, what that looks like, I'm still learning that. I know I need to acknowledge the pain, let go of the hurt, remember God's forgiveness, continue to forgive, and pray for the person who hurt me. So, I'll go through those steps every day until I "feel" it.

"You shall not take vengeance, nor hear any grudge against the children of your people, but you shall love your neighbor as yourself; I am the Lord."

Leviticus 19:18

For this, I will put aside my grudge and grace others with the mercy God shows me.

What is not found in Scripture, is the phrase "forgive and forget". Scripture says that God will remove our transgressions from us (Psalm 103:12) and He will wash us white as snow (Isaiah 1:18) through Christ's shed blood on the cross. Humans are not able to do this perfectly like God does.

However, Scripture does say that love keeps no record of wrongs, and that love conquers a multitude of sins. But does this mean you simply forget the sin committed against you? That's tough.

Christ's atoning work on the cross perfectly covers all your past, current, and future sins. So, any pain you have dealt with in the past, are dealing with in the present, or will deal with in the future is perfectly cared for by Jesus. The gospel frees you up! You have been forgiven so you are able to forgive (Col. 3:13, 2 Cor. 5:18-19).

So, is 'forgetting' biblical? No, it is not. But God perfectly models what forgiveness entails through Christ. You are called to walk in the power that is extended to you through his mercy. To let the pain from a past hurt or offense keep you from walking in healing is to misunderstand the all-encompassing work of the gospel to save, sanctify, and glorify us.

Forgive others, not because they deserve forgiveness, but because you deserve peace. And forget the pain, but never the lessons you gained.

Reviews

"As a woman who has gone through a lot of what Monaca has, I found after reading her book that I would have benefitted tremendously had I had something like this to help me. If you're presently experiencing any of these situations, then you know how alone you feel because nobody is walking in your shoes but you. Who do you talk to? Who can guide you? After reading this book, you'll have more strength and resolve to advocate for yourself and walk away from a toxic relationship. I would recommend this book to anyone struggling in a relationship."

~ Anonymous

" 'Jokers Dressed Up as Kings' is a captivating book that uncovers the reality behind a seemingly flawless relationship. With brutal honesty and through raw and unflinching storytelling, Monaca peels back the facade of her picture-perfect life, exposing the intricate web of lies, manipulation, and broken promises that festered behind closed doors. Monaca invites readers into her world, revealing the hidden layers of deception and shattered vows. Her story is not just her own, but a mirror for others to recognize and find hope illuminating the path towards healing and empowerment amid narcissistic turmoil."

~ Sasha

"An incredible, witty, and creative writer. Relationships are tough and Monaca helped me understand why I was always blaming myself and didn't recognize the missteps by my partner."

~ Demi

" 'Jokers Dressed Up as Kings' is an exhilarating book that will resonate with anyone who has experienced the destructive effects of narcissism. The author's compassionate and insightful approach offers hope and practical solutions for those seeking to break free from the cycle of narcissism and embark on a journey of self-discovery and healing."

~ Chanel

"Sometimes we can't see the forest through the trees. Monaca's book is one of resilience, learning and uncovering. Most individuals don't realize they are involved in a narcissistic relationship until they are out of it. By reading her story of the raw truth hopefully you can see the signs sooner than she did and give you the strength to leave any relationship you don't love yourself in."

~ Anna

Dear Gentle Reader- To say this read made me laugh, cry, and cuss, sounds a little cliche. However, all of the former happened....

REPEATEDLY.

"Jokers Dressed up as Kings feels more like relaxed convos and cocktails with Monaca. She bares her soul as uniquely as the spelling of her name with the prayer being that it shines a light so others may see and save themselves. She illuminates red flags that others may not see as red flags. She illuminates abuse that all may not realize is abuse. However maybe most importantly, she illuminates that it is NOT the desire of God, to have the people of God, out of the will of God. As such, this book acts as a toxic relationship decoder map complete with definitions and BIBLICAL BACKUP! Jokers Dressed up as Kings hits the jackpot and should be standard reading for us all. Whether you feel you may be in a toxic relationship, love someone in a toxic relationship, don't realize you are in a toxic relationship, or just want a short entertaining & educational read, have this little gem as an ace up your sleeve."

Lady Johnson
Copley, OH

124

GLITCH MOB PODCAST

WHERE REAL STORIES, INSIGHTS, AND CONVERSATIONS COME TO LIFE. JOIN YOUR HOST, MONACA VANDERPOOL, A SINGLE MOM, ENTREPRENEUR, AND A BELIEVER IN THE POWER OF RESILIENCE AND TRANSFORMATION. AT GLITCH MOB, WE TEAR OFF THE VEIL OF PERFECTION TO SHARE THE RAW, THE REAL, AND THE TRULY LIFE-CHANGING STORIES. WHETHER YOU'RE A SINGLE PARENT, A BUDDING ENTREPRENEUR, OR SOMEONE WHO'S SIMPLY SEEKING INSPIRATION AMIDST LIFE'S CHAOS, YOU'VE FOUND YOUR TRIBE. WE'LL CHAT WITH INCREDIBLE GUESTS, SHARE ACTIONABLE INSIGHTS, AND, MOST IMPORTANTLY, WE'LL DO IT TOGETHER, AS A COMMUNITY THAT UPLIFTS AND EMPOWERS. IT'S TIME TO EMBRACE THE GLITCH AND FIND THE BEAUTY IN THE BREAKDOWNS.

WWW.MONACAVANDERPOOL.COM

WITH MONACA VANDERPOOL

About the Author

Monaca Vanderpool's journey is a testament to resilience, faith, and the entrepreneurial spirit. Born in Frankfurt, Germany, Monaca grew up in a military family, which instilled in her a sense of discipline and adaptability from a young age. After graduating cum laude with a degree in Business Administration, she discovered her passion for marketing and sales, a field that perfectly suited her outgoing personality.

After the birth of her first child and the dissolution of her marriage, life took an unexpected turn when Monaca's house was destroyed by a tornado, prompting her to move back home to Virginia. This challenging period did not deter her from building her new life; instead, it fueled her determination.

As a single mother, Monaca made the bold decision to leave a secure job and dive into a commission-only sales role with a promotional company. Realizing she was passionate about business, Monaca founded her own promotional products company, which thrived under her leadership and surpassed $1 million in sales.

Monaca's entrepreneurial journey continued as she established two other successful businesses in the following decade. Throughout her entrepreneurial ventures, Monaca learned the invaluable lesson of "letting go to grow," and trusting in the right connections to help her build her dreams. Her unwavering work ethic and ability to align herself with the right people have been pivotal in her success.

Amid her professional achievements, Monaca faced personal adversities, including the end of a thirteen-year toxic relationship, an unexpected health diagnosis, and navigating the realities of single parenthood. As Monaca began to heal and untangle herself from the unhealthy dynamics of her past, she felt inspired to write this book to help others recognize the traits of narcissistic abuse in their own lives.

Her experiences also motivated her to create The Glitch Mob Podcast, a platform dedicated to sharing stories of resilience, self-love, and empowerment. Through the podcast, Monaca explores the importance of self-care, drawing on her own life and business lessons, such as stepping out in faith, grieving the loss of relationships, and creating the life you know you were meant for.

Monaca's story is not just about business success; it's about faith, family, and the relentless pursuit of purpose. For her, purpose comes from providing an abundant life to her children, who are the center of her world. When Monaca is not pursuing her next business venture she loves traveling, reading, staying fit, and spending time with her two French bulldogs Rip and Roxy. Monaca's life is a powerful narrative of overcoming obstacles, trusting in divine nudges, and inspiring others to find beauty in their breakdowns.

References

- ❖ Wikipedia
- ❖ Oxford Dictionary
- ❖ Charlie Health
- ❖ Narcissist Family Files
- ❖ The Good Men Project
- ❖ Narcissistic Abuse Rehab
- ❖ WebMD
- ❖ Psych Central
- ❖ Medicine Net
- ❖ Cleveland Clinic Health Essentials
- ❖ World Population Review
- ❖ The Hotline (.org)
- ❖ Medical News Today
- ❖ Got Questions (.org)

Made in the USA
Columbia, SC
22 August 2024

40954340R00076